How to Find Your Divine Spouse
TWO SPIRITS COMING INTO ONE SPIRIT

DAVID L. ROBERSON, D.Min

TWO SPIRITS COMING INTO ONE SPIRIT

DAVID L. ROBERSON, D.Min

*Priority*ONE
publications
Detroit, MI USA

How to Find Your Divine Spouse:
Two Spirits Coming into One Spirit
Copyright © 2025 David L. Roberson, D.Min.

Unless otherwise indicated, all Scripture quotations are taken from the Holy Bible, New King James Version®. Copyright © 1982 by Thomas Nelson. Used by permission. All rights reserved.

Scripture quotations marked (NLT) are taken from the *Holy Bible*, New Living Translation, copyright ©1996, 2004, 2015 by Tyndale House Foundation. Used by permission of Tyndale House Publishers, Carol Stream, Illinois 60188. All rights reserved.

Scripture quotations marked from the Amplified® Bible (AMP), Copyright © 2015 by The Lockman Foundation. Used by permission. Lockman.org

All rights reserved. No part of this publication may be reproduced, stored in a retrieval system, or transmitted in any form or by any means – electronic, mechanical, photocopy, recording, or any other – except for brief quotations in printed reviews without the prior permission of the publisher.

*Priority*ONE Publications
P. O. Box 361332 | Grosse Pointe, MI 48236
E-mail: info@priorityonebooks.com
URL: http://www.priorityonebooks.com

PRINT BOOK
ISBN 13:   978-1-933972-82-3
ISBN 10:   1-933972-82-4

EBOOK
ISBN 13:   978-1-933972-83-1
ISBN 10:   1-933972-83-1

Editing by Patricia Hicks
Cover Design by Thomas Crump
Interior design by Christina Dixon

Printed in the United States of America

Table of Contents

Dedication 7
Foreword 9
Chapter One: The Foundation of Divine Love 13
Chapter Two: The Biblical Basis for Finding Your Spouse 17
Chapter Three: Finding My Spouse with Divine Guidance 21
Chapter Four: The Significance of Marriage and Finding a Spouse in the Black Community 37
Chapter Five: Traits, Characteristics, and Features to Consider in Finding a Spouse 41
Chapter Six: Embracing One Another Before Marriage 49
Chapter Seven: Summation of Benefits in Waiting for YOUR Spouse 55
Chapter Eight: Seven Steps to Find Your Spouse from God 59
Author Bio 67

Dedication

This book is dedicated to everyone who desires to have a life-long marriage with someone who has been divinely chosen just for them.

I also dedicate it to Cathy, my wife of over forty years, who has made my life richer for her presence in it. I am so glad that God chose her for me.

To God, by Whose wisdom and guidance I was led to be honest about what mattered most to me as I sought a mate. To Him be all the glory!

Foreword

I have had the joy and privilege of knowing Pastor Roberson and his beautiful wife, Catherine, for over three decades. Our connection began through the ministry of Biblical Counseling, where Pastor Roberson's unwavering commitment to sharing the profound truth of God's Word first drew me in. Over the years, I have witnessed his passion for encouraging others to not only learn the scriptures but to live them out in their daily lives.

It was on a sunny, radiant day in Miami—while my husband, Deacon Jose, and I were savoring the warmth of a well-earned vacation—that Pastor Roberson invited us to join him and Catherine for lunch at a charming restaurant by the pier. The sun shone brightly overhead, casting its golden rays as if to bless the day with enchantment. With her gentle grace and radiant smile, Catherine looked as if the world had paused while her husband shared his admiration for her. As we sat there, the air filled with the soft sounds of the waves and the distant hum of life around us, Pastor Roberson began to speak of the book he was working on—a work on marriage and the journey of finding your divine spouse. His words painted a picture so vivid, so full of life and love, that they seemed to float before me like a dream.

At that moment, I couldn't help but think that *Jose and I may be the world's power couple, love birds in our own right,* but Pastor Roberson's vision? He had flown to another realm of love that was as exciting as it was eternal. The story he was about to share would captivate anyone who had ever dared to dream of a love transcending time and circumstance. I knew then that I would write the foreword for this inspiring work.

The scriptures teach us that a thriving relationship with God is the bedrock upon which a divine marriage can flourish. By seeking God first and aligning ourselves with His purpose, He leads us to a partner who shares the same spiritual foundation. Our relationships testify to His love and faithfulness as we build our lives on the Rock of Ages.

In our quest for a divine spouse, we must recognize the profound importance of establishing an intimate and strong relationship with God first. This foundation is not merely a prerequisite—it is the cornerstone that shapes the entire structure of a divine union. In seeking God for a partner, we are following the timeless wisdom embedded in biblical truth that Pastor Roberson outlines in sections titled: *The Lord is my Shepherd, Delight Thyself in the Lord, Two are better than one, Be ye equally yoked.*

Pastor Roberson tells the story of how he embarked on his journey of seeking a partner. He listed the qualities he desired in the mate he would one day marry and then articulated his heartfelt longings to the Divine, trusting that God would guide him to the mate He had designed for him. God did it and fulfilled the deepest desires of Pastor Roberson's heart.

Clearly, God answered his prayers. Pastor David Roberson's 40 years of marriage are a testament to God's faithfulness in love and partnership. Now, he shares his vision of divine light in print, offering sage advice for those who desire to be married and for those who may need to remember the dream that once connected them to the one they love. Pastor Roberson's insights are a gift for those who seek clarity and wisdom in their own journeys, as well as for those who need a renewed reminder of the dream that led them to each other.

As you turn these pages, ask yourself: *Have you truly sought the guidance of the One who knows the desires of your heart?* Chapter 8 is worth the wait—though if you're eager, you'll find a wonderful summation of the entire book in its pages.

Just as God formed Eve for Adam, He formed Catherine for Pastor David Roberson. And in the same way, He has formed someone in His image just for you—a partner who will align with your dreams and your calling. This person will be everything you've longed for, just as if you had designed him or her yourself. God knows the desires of your heart and what you need in a mate to move into your next assignment—marriage.

It is my joy to introduce you to the wisdom within these pages, which will undoubtedly guide you toward the divine union you were always meant to have.

Dr. Sabrina D. Black,
Author, Counselor, International Speaker
Can Two Walk Together
Live Right Now

Chapter One:
The Foundation of Divine Love

In the quest for a divine spouse, one must recognize the profound importance of establishing a strong and intimate relationship with God first. This foundation is not just a mere prerequisite but a crucial cornerstone that shapes the entire structure of a divine union. The wisdom of seeking God before seeking a life partner is deeply embedded in biblical teachings.

Seek Ye First the Kingdom of God

In the Gospel, according to Matthew 6:33 (King James Version), Jesus imparts a timeless truth: *"But seek ye first the kingdom of God, and his righteousness, and all these things shall be added unto you."* That includes your spouse. This verse emphasizes the prioritization of our relationship with God above all else. By establishing a solid connection with the divine, we align ourselves with God's will, ensuring His wisdom and grace guide our pursuits. What can stop you from aligning yourself with God's purpose for your life? May I suggest goals, people, professions, and many other objectives? All these things compete for first place in your life. You must actively choose to give God first place in all areas of your life. What is most important to you? You must decide, or all the other things competing for your attention will take over and become first place in your life.

The Lord is My Shepherd

Psalm 23:1 echoes the sentiment of a deep and personal relationship with God: *"The Lord is my shepherd; I shall not want."* In recognizing God as our shepherd, we acknowledge His role as the guide and provider in our lives. A well-established relationship with God serves as a source of comfort, guidance, and fulfillment, laying the groundwork for a harmonious partnership with a divine spouse. The Bible describes the Lord as our Shepherd, sheep are completely dependent upon the Shepherd for guidance, provision, and protection. This passage of scripture does not focus on the animal-like qualities of sheep but on the discipleship qualities of those who are willing to follow the good shepherd where He leads. The New Testament calls Jesus the good shepherd in John 10:11, the great Shepherd in Hebrews 13:20, and the Chief Shepherd in 1. 1 Peter 5:4.

Delight Thyself in the Lord

Psalm 37:4 (KJV) further encourages the invitation of a profound connection with God: *"Delight thyself also in the Lord, and he shall give thee the desires of thine heart."* Delighting in the Lord involves finding joy and satisfaction in His presence. As we immerse ourselves in God's love and truth, our desires align with His purpose, paving the way for a divine partner who shares in this spiritual alignment. The most important thing is that you get your relationship right with God. The Bible is filled with scripture that states that God wants to bless you. He wants to give you the desires of your heart, and He knows the plans that He has for you. Jeremiah 29:11(NLT): *"For I know the plans I have for you, says the Lord. They are plans for good and not for disaster, to give you a future and a hope."* This is in harmony with the Apostle John in 3 John 1:2 that he *"...wishes, above all things, that you prosper and be in good health."* That includes having a life partner that certainly spurs on all these things. Once you have the right relationship with God, you have to make a pledge to God that you are going to wait for God before going out on your own seeking a soulmate or your life partner. Recognize that you don't have all the tools needed because if you did, you would have already done so. Because of that, you're willing to wait patiently for God to show you the way to go.

Two Are Better Than One

"9 Two are better than one,

Because they have a good reward for their labor.

10 For if they fall, one will lift up his companion.

But woe to him who is alone when he falls,

For he has no one to help him up.

11 Again, if two lie down together, they will keep warm;

But how can one be warm alone?

12 Though one may be overpowered by another, two can withstand him.

And a threefold cord is not quickly broken."

Ecclesiastes 4:9-12

The scripture reflects the strength found in a union grounded in God: *"Two are better than one; because they have a good reward for their labor... a threefold cord is not quickly broken."* This passage underscores the significance of involving God as the third strand in the cord of a relationship. When both individuals are individually anchored in their relationship with God, the bond becomes resilient, with the divine at its core.

Having a spouse has its advantages; you are not alone, nor are you isolated. Isolation is preferred by some who think they will not trust anyone. Don't isolate yourself trying to go it alone. Be a team member because you have companionship with a spouse.

Be Equally Yoked

In 2 Corinthians 6:14 (KJV), the Apostle Paul provides guidance on the importance of spiritual compatibility in relationships: *"Be ye not unequally yoked together with unbelievers: for what fellowship hath righteousness with unrighteousness?"* Being equally yoked means sharing a common commitment to God, ensuring that both partners are moving in the same spiritual direction. This principle emphasizes that a solid foundation in faith is fundamental for a lasting and God-honoring union. This scripture has a strong application to marriage. Believers should not enter into marriage with unbelievers since such a marriage cannot have unity with the important issues in life, and it is a commitment to follow God in obedience to His word.

In conclusion, the scriptures teach us that a thriving relationship with God is the bedrock upon which a divine marriage can flourish. By seeking God first, we align ourselves with His purpose, allowing Him to lead us to a partner who shares the same spiritual foundation. As we build our lives on the Rock of Ages, our relationships become a testament to His love and faithfulness.

Chapter Two:

The Biblical Basis for Finding Your Spouse

The search for a life partner is a significant journey, and for those seeking guidance, the Bible provides a solid foundation for the principles and values that should guide this pursuit. The New King James Version offers timeless wisdom that illuminates the biblical basis for finding a spouse. In finding a spouse, your decisions should be guided by your faith and relationship with God. There are no step-by-step instructions in the Bible for finding a spouse. However, the Bible does offer some principles and values that many Christians consider when seeking a spouse. The following are some biblical bases for finding a spouse.

God's Plan for Companionship

In Genesis 2:18, *"And the Lord God said, 'It is not good that man should be alone; I will make him a helper comparable to him."* Here, we find the inception of the divine plan for companionship. This verse underscores the importance of companionship and the divine intention behind creating a suitable partner. The search for a spouse is rooted in God's design for human relationships. God's creative work for the human race was not complete until He made woman, and in so doing, He chose to make her from man's flesh and bone, illustrating for us that in marriage, man and woman symbolically are united into one. Throughout the Bible, God treats marriage partnership seriously. If you plan to be married, are you willing to keep the commitment that makes the two of you one? The goal in marriage is oneness.

Trust in the Lord's Guidance

Proverbs 3:5-6 Implores us to trust in the Lord's guidance in all aspects of life, including the search for a life partner: ***"Trust in the Lord with all your heart, and lean not on your own understanding; In all your ways acknowledge Him, and He shall direct your paths."*** This verse is a powerful affirmation that seeking God's guidance in finding a spouse is essential, acknowledging that His wisdom surpasses our own. God knows what is best for us; He is a better judge of what we want than we are! We must trust God completely in every choice we make. We must always be willing to listen and be corrected by God's Word and His wise counsel. Bring your decisions to God in prayer, use the Bible as your guide, and then follow God's leading.

The Beauty of Patience

In Psalm 27:14, ***"Wait on the Lord; be of good courage, and He shall strengthen your heart; wait, I say, on the Lord!"*** The journey to find a life partner may require patience, but through trust in God's timing, we are strengthened, and our hearts find courage in the assurance of His perfect plan. Sometimes, waiting on God is not easy. There are times when we feel that He is not answering our prayers or that He does not understand the urgency of our request. Clearly, God is worth waiting for. Make good use of your waiting because many times, God uses waiting to renew, refresh, and teach us something.

Seek Righteousness in a Partner

Proverbs 31:10: ***"Who can find a virtuous wife? For her worth is far above rubies."*** This verse emphasizes the importance of seeking a partner whose character aligns with the values of righteousness and virtue, recognizing that true worth surpasses material considerations. This scripture extols the value of a virtuous and righteous spouse. The Bible presents this woman as an excellent wife and mother. She is also a manufacturer, importer, manager, realtor, farmer, seamstress, upholsterer, and merchant. All these characteristics are a result of her reverence for God. Who can find such a woman? All things are possible with God.

Prayer for Discernment

Philippians 1:9-10 provides a powerful affirmation for prayer in the pursuit of a life partner: *"And this I pray, that your love may abound still more and more in knowledge and all discernment, that you may approve the things that are excellent, that you may be sincere and without offense till the day of Christ."* Through prayer, we seek discernment in choosing a partner whose love and character align with God's standards. The verse provides a powerful affirmation for prayer in the pursuit of a life partner.

Affirmation

I trust in the Lord's perfect plan for my life, including the journey to find a life partner. I patiently wait for His guidance, seeking a companion whose virtues reflect the righteousness and love that God values. I commit my desires to Him, knowing that He will direct my paths and grant me the desires of my heart according to His will.

In summary, the biblical basis for finding a spouse is anchored in God's plan for companionship: trust in His guidance, patience, seeking righteousness, and fervent prayer for discernment. By aligning our search with these principles, we embrace a journey that reflects God's wisdom and leads to a union blessed by His divine hand.

Chapter Three:

Finding My Spouse with Divine Guidance

In this chapter, I will recount the remarkable journey of discovering my life partner, guided by the benevolence of God. My faith has always been an integral part of my existence, nurtured since my childhood in a devout household where attending Sunday school and church was non-negotiable. This foundation in faith played a pivotal role in my quest for love.

As I embarked on this journey, I discovered solace in the scriptures. Over 69 verses in the Bible spoke to God's promise of granting the desires of our hearts, the hopes we hold dear, and the wishes we cherish. These divine assurances gave me the courage to dream again.

However, my path to love had its share of trials. I had experienced a failed marriage, which understandably left me cautious about reentering the sacred covenant of matrimony. In this trying period, I turned to God in prayer, earnestly seeking His guidance in my pursuit of a loving and supportive spouse. I desired a partner who would stand by my side without criticism but with unwavering encouragement.

To better communicate my heart's desires to God, I began to list the attributes I hoped to find in the woman I would marry. Though it may sound like I was designing the perfect spouse, this list was my way of articulating my heartfelt longings to the Divine.

Let's review some of the criteria that I set forth:

Physical Attractiveness

I prayed for a beautiful wife, understanding that physical attraction is an important aspect of a romantic relationship. I imagined myself awakening in the morning to a face that I really didn't approve of, and I didn't think that would be a lasting relationship. When I met Cathy, her face was beautiful to me. Her eyes were bright and expressive, which seemed to express emotions to me. Her skin was smooth and flawless. When we were out on a date, people would come over and ask her what country she was from. Are you from Colombia, or are you from someplace other than that? All of this would express beauty to me. She had a pretty face that described what I always wanted to awaken to every morning, and after all of these years, I still awaken to her beautiful face. I would watch her walk, and the way she carried herself was all beautiful to me.

Educational Achievement

I wished for a spouse with at least a bachelor's degree, but I received a remarkable woman with a doctorate and multiple degrees. Education reveals a mindset that searches for the importance of hard work, discipline, and long-term goal setting. I had various goals in mind and needed a partner with a degree that would align with my own aspirations. Certainly, when I met Cathy, she fulfilled all of those goals for me. Also, I thought that education was very important in rearing children. I also thought that having a person with whom I could communicate on a higher educational level would sustain our relationship in seeking goals together; I found the perfect person in Cathy.

Employment

It was imperative for me that my future spouse be gainfully employed, independent, and self-sufficient rather than relying on someone else for financial stability. Being employed, in my mind, would mean that she could contribute to the household financially, which would ease the stress in our home. Her employment will allow both of us to share the burdens of bills, savings, and future goals instead of everything being a strain on me. It also means that she was confident and independent, contributing positively to her own well-being as well as to our well-being. What I'm trying to say is that we would both share the responsibilities of maintaining a home, rearing our children, and retiring together, which was very important to me. My wife's work would create a more equal balance in our relationship, which would foster mutual respect, understanding, and support. It would minimize any power imbalance that arises when one person feels financially dependent upon the other, which I did not want.

Culinary Skills

I desired a wife who could cook, recognizing the age-old saying that "the way to a man's heart is through his stomach." When I grew up as a kid, I had a week to cook breakfast and a week to cook dinner. It was so important to me that I found a wife who had the ability to cook. While dating Cathy, she would visit me over the weekend, and she would always cook and leave my house with the refrigerator filled with food for me to eat for the remainder of the week. She demonstrated that she had many culinary skills, which I enjoyed so much, having come from a home where my mother and father would cook. I wanted a wife who could cook along with me as I cooked, and that is what I found in Cathy.

Cleanliness

I wanted assurance that she could maintain a clean home, which I discovered when visiting her. Growing up as a kid, I had a week to clean the kitchen, the living room, the dining room, and the bathrooms. I always had to keep my room clean. My mother would come and examine the kitchen after I had washed dishes, and from that experience, I would have to do the floors over, clean the stove down again, and wipe the refrigerator down again. I learned cleanliness from my home growing up as a kid. When I visited Cathy, I would make certain that her place was clean by checking when I would go to the bathroom. I would feel the face bowl to see if it was clean or not. When hanging my coat in her closet, I would check the floors to see if they were junked up or were really clean. The way she maintained her home was very clean. Also, when she visited me over the weekend, she would mop the floors because she would say my house was dirty. I said, to my surprise, I found a woman who cleans better than I. It was all beautiful to me. She was a very clean person. There's so much more I could say, but for now, I'll just stop.

Family Values

I wanted a spouse who came from a loving and close-knit family, which was another essential requirement, as family held great importance in my life. I was looking for a partner who prioritizes and shares the same beliefs as I did and whose family values encompassed qualities like commitment, respect, communication, and shared goals. Cathy's family values included traditions, religion, and culture. She was able to communicate openly and effectively, which was important to me. She was able to show emotional support to me, which made me know she would stand by her family members and offer help and encouragement when needed. It was important to find someone whose vision for family aligned with my vision of how we would spend time together and raise our children. I was seeking a partner who views marriage as a lifelong partnership based on trust, mutual respect, and love, which was crucial to me in building a stable family.

Independence

Having her own transportation was crucial to me, as I valued a partner with the freedom to come and go as she pleased. Having her own transportation demonstrated independence, which, to me, was a healthy aspect of a balanced relationship. It speaks first to her ability to maintain her individuality, make decisions for herself, and contribute to our partnership in her own way while also being a team member. This was very important to me. An emotionally independent wife would be confident in her own worth, making her less likely to rely upon me for validation. This independence would enable her to pursue her own interests, hobbies, and goals outside of the relationship. This would encourage growth not just for her but for us. It would also allow her to continue evolving as an individual, which can positively influence our relationship.

Financial Responsibility

I prayed for someone with good credit, as it reflected their financial responsibility. Financial independence would allow her to not only contribute to the household responsibilities while making her own decisions and feeling empowered, all of which can help her maintain a sense of self. This is what I mean when I say creditworthiness. In a relationship where both parties are independent, this is often a healthier balance of power and respect. Independence helps prevent codependence, where one partner relies too heavily on the other for emotional and financial support. This balance brings mutual respect, individual autonomy, and an interesting understanding that both people can thrive in their own way.

Harmonious Relationships

A spouse who would get along with my family and respect my parents was paramount. I was seeking a partner with whom I could have a mutually harmonious relationship, who would value my opinions, boundaries, and individuality just as I would do the same in return; a respectful partner who listens without judgment and acknowledges each other's differences with understanding. Effective communication is essential for a harmonious relationship. A wife who expresses herself clearly and listens attentively helps create an environment where both parties and their extended families can share their thoughts, feelings, and concerns openly. This reduces misunderstanding and helps resolve conflict more easily. I got along so well with Cathy. We both worked for the state of Michigan. We went to work together, we ate lunch together, and we came home together. My friends would ask me why I wouldn't have lunch with them. I would take her picture from my wallet and show it to them. Then, ask, "Who would you rather have lunch with?" They all said nothing.

Acceptance and Love

I wished for a spouse who would love me unconditionally, even if I enjoyed a glass of wine in the evening. Cathy accepted me wholeheartedly. We were honest and open with our feelings and thoughts, which promoted balance, and we both valued that in our lives. Honest communication helps prevent misunderstandings and shows that both individuals are committed to respecting each other's feelings and perspectives, which is mutual and essential. She would listen attentively emphatically, and she was accepting. If I decided to have a glass of wine, she would have a glass of wine with me. She would go to a movie with me if I wanted to go to a movie. If I wanted to play cards, she would play cards with me. When I met Cathy, she didn't play the card game Pinochle, but she willingly learned how to play. She would play with me, and I saw that as her accepting me wholeheartedly. She was with me no matter what I wanted to do or where I wanted to go. She was saying count me in, and that's what acceptance is to me. To be accepting of someone, you have to love them.

Commitment

Most importantly, I desired a spouse who would be committed to our journey together until death parted us. While seeking a wife who would demonstrate commitment, I looked for qualities that showed that she was dedicated to both the relationship and our shared future. Commitment in a marriage goes beyond just saying I do or staying together. It reflects loyalty, trust, effort, and shared responsibility. While working with Cathy on many political campaigns and community efforts, these qualities showed me she was a loyal partner who stood by me through thick and thin. She remained faithful and prioritized our relationship. I saw trustworthiness in her; I saw a committed wife. I saw someone I wanted to spend the rest of my life with. She kept her promises, she was reliable, and she acted with integrity. I trusted her, and I'm thankful for her.

But how did I know that God was truly answering my prayers and guiding me to the right partner? It was when I met a woman who embodied most of the qualities I had fervently prayed for. It was then that I knew, with unwavering certainty, that God was directing me toward my life partner, not just a spouse.

How I Met My Wonderful Wife

Allow me to recount the remarkable story of our first encounter and what followed.

On September 15th, 1978, a friend invited me to watch a boxing match called **"The Battle of New Orleans."** The exact fighters escape my memory, but what I do remember is an unexpected turn of fate. My friend asked me to pick up his sister-in-law on my way to the event. Little did I know that this meeting would alter the course of my life forever.

As I arrived at the gathering, everyone was engrossed in the impending fight, which began around 10:45 PM. I gradually met each person present, and it was when I met Cathy that time seemed to stand still. Meeting her felt like an indelible moment when the world ceased to turn, and my life was profoundly impacted. Her presence left a lasting mark on my soul.

I must confess that my initial attempts to contact her faltered, and I lost her phone number. It took two weeks for my friend to return from vacation before I could retrieve her number and make that fateful call. The stakes were high, as I felt an inexplicable connection with her from our brief meeting.

However, God's intervention in our love story extends beyond the earthly realm. An extraordinary spiritual experience solidified our destiny as soulmates. I found myself at a crossroads, struggling with doubts and temptations. I attended a party alone, pondering the idea of ending our budding relationship. In a state of inebriation, I returned home, only to awaken in a different room, inexplicably disrobed. It was a disorienting experience.

The following day, a phone call changed the course of my life. Pastor Harris urgently requested my presence. I confessed my joblessness and lack of transportation, expecting this to end our conversation. Yet, someone miraculously appeared to pick me up, and I soon found myself at Pastor Harris's side.

Pastor Harris shared his dream from the previous night in a conversation that I will forever hold in my heart. He described seeing me running away from a woman, utterly disrobed. This vivid dream piqued my interest as it aligned strangely with my bewildering night.

Pastor Harris then advised me to go home, kneel in prayer, and ask God to reveal His plan for my life. I heeded this counsel with a humble heart and sincere intention.

What followed was nothing short of a divine encounter:

As I knelt in prayer, I heard a voice in the darkness of my room urging me to cease my supplications. It was a mysterious presence, a voice that seemed otherworldly, and it instructed me not to pray. Perplexed, I questioned its origin. It persisted, yet I, in turn, called upon the indwelling spirit within me, declaring my intention to remain in prayer until God answered.

This inner dialogue escalated into a fervent communion with God, a dialogue in which I proclaimed my unity with the Father and articulated my desire to be one with Him. While I cannot recall every word spoken in that divine conversation, it echoed with an intensity that rivaled the biblical verses I had clung to for guidance.

And then, a surreal experience unfolded:

I found myself in my bedroom, flying above my own body, circling it as it lay motionless on the bed. Astonished, I observed a spiritual presence occupying my physical form, draped in a robe emitting ethereal light. Two beams of light emanated from this spiritual figure's wrists, and an even brighter glow radiated from a wound in its side.

Intriguingly, I noticed another spiritual presence, Cathy's essence, coexisting within my body. My spiritual counterpart and I stood face-to-face, sharing an inexplicable connection. Our unity transcended the physical realm as the spiritual figure within me breathed life into both of us.

What followed was an unmistakable baptism, as if our souls had been inextricably intertwined. The spiritual presence then departed, ascended through the wall, and returned to the heavenly realm. While I recognized that more than one entity was present, I was captivated by this singular figure.

In that profound moment, I knew without a shadow of a doubt that Cathy was destined to be my wife. However, the challenge lay in rekindling our connection, for I had lost contact with her, and uncertainty clouded my heart.

Miraculously, our paths converged once more:

Despite my initial struggles to reconnect with Cathy, I persisted in my pursuit. I called her repeatedly, only to be met with her absence. It was then that her father, having witnessed my relentless efforts, instructed her to answer the phone.

When she finally picked up the call, I invited her to accompany me to church. She agreed, and together, we attended an 8:00 AM service. The pastor's words during the sermon resonated deeply with me as he spoke about the importance of honoring and committing to one's partner.

Turning to Cathy, I conveyed my conviction that I needed to join the church, as the preacher's words felt directly aimed at me. She hesitated, expressing her reservations about joining a Baptist church. Yet, I decided to take the step alone, leaving my seat and walking down the aisle.

Something inexplicable occurred as I walked down that aisle. I don't recall the physical steps, but it was as if some unseen force guided me. I found myself seated in a chair, my head buried in my hands, wrestling with my thoughts about our uncertain future. But when I opened my eyes, I was met with a sight that filled me with hope and love—Cathy sat beside me.

Overwhelmed by emotion, I asked her what had changed her mind. She shared that an irresistible spiritual force had come over her, compelling her to join me in this pivotal moment.

We became engaged in that divine space, a testament to the power of faith, prayer, and an unbreakable connection. It was an unmistakable sign from God that our union was preordained.

Fast-forward to over 40 years of marriage. It is indisputable that our love story was divinely orchestrated. Our union, second only to accepting Jesus as our Savior, has been a journey filled with joy, love, and fulfillment. We have become one in every sense of the word, where our thoughts and words are seamlessly entwined.

Sage Advice

I must confess that when it came to my daughter's pursuit of love and marriage, I offered her (and you) some sage advice:

The A-List and B-List:

I urged her to discern between individuals on her "A-list," those she enjoys being around but may not reciprocate her feelings, and those on her "B-list," individuals who may not initially meet all her criteria but possess the potential to grow into the ideal partner.

Love Over Perfection

I emphasized that no one is perfect, and it's essential to focus on finding someone who loves and supports her, even if they don't align perfectly with her checklist. Love has the power to nurture and grow a relationship.

Open Communication

I stressed the importance of open and honest communication in any relationship. Sharing desires, expectations, and concerns is key to building a strong foundation.

Prayer and a Clean Heart

Just as my journey was marked by faith and sincere prayer, I encouraged my daughter to approach the quest for love with a clean heart and a connection to the divine.

Helping Each Other Grow

I reminded her that no one is static; we all have room to grow. If her potential partner doesn't meet all her criteria initially, she has the power to help them evolve into the ideal spouse. She has been married for fourteen years now and has two kids. She listed what she was looking for in a spouse, took it before the Lord, and prayed and prayed. I would hear her upstairs in her room praying to God, and God answered her prayer with a young man who had all the features she was looking for in a spouse.

My story is a testament to the profound impact of faith, prayer, and divine guidance in pursuing love. I encourage you, dear reader, to embark on your own journey guided by faith. You've explored various avenues and events in search of the perfect partner, but have you truly sought the guidance of the One who knows the desires of your heart?

I challenge you to approach God with an open heart, laying your desires before Him. He has promised to fulfill the desires of your heart, and He already has a plan for you. Allow Him to guide your path and work His divine design. Seek His presence in your prayers, just as I did, and you may find that your journey to love and marriage is divinely ordained.

In closing my story, I want to share some of the scriptures that strengthened my faith and fortified my resolve on this journey:

(Psalm 37:4-6 AMP)

4"Delight yourself also in the Lord, and He will give you the desires and secret petitions of your heart. 5Committ your way to the Lord [roll and repose each care of your load on Him]; trust (lean on, rely on, and be confident) also in Him and He will bring it to pass. 6 And He will make your uprightness and right standing with God go forth as the light, and your justice and right as [the shining sun of] the noon day."

Psalm 145:18-19 AMP

" *The Lord is near to all who call upon Him, to all who call upon Him sincerely and in truth. 19 He will fulfill the desires of those who reverently and worshipfully fear Him; He also will hear their cry and will save them.*"

John 15:7 AMP

"*If you live in Me [abide vitally united to Me] and My words remain in you and continue to live in your hearts, ask whatever you will, and it shall be done for you.*"

Matthew 7:7-8 AMP

7 "Keep on asking and it will be given you; keep on seeking and you will find: keep on knocking [reverently] and [the door] will be opened to you. 8 For everyone who keeps on asking receives: and he who keeps on seeking finds: and to him who keeps on knocking, [the door] will be opened."

Psalm 20:4 AMP

"*May He grant you according to your heart's desire and fulfill all your plans.*"

Remember, you are not alone on this quest. God is with you every step of the way, ready to guide your heart toward the love you desire. Countless individuals have followed this path and found the love and companionship they sought. May your journey be blessed, and may you find the love your heart longs for.

Chapter Four:
The Significance of Marriage and Finding a Spouse in the Black Community

Within our present culture and society, the institution of marriage holds profound importance, serving as a cornerstone for the stability and growth of individuals and communities. In the context of the Black community, marriage's significance is deeply rooted in historical, cultural, and biblical foundations, offering a framework for shared values, resilience, and empowerment.

Historical Legacy and Cultural Connection

The Black community has a rich historical legacy that emphasizes the strength found in familial bonds. Marriage, within this context, is a continuation of a tradition that has withstood the challenges of time. It is a testament to resilience and unity that has been essential for progress and empowerment.

Empowerment through Family Structure

Marriage provides a stable foundation for family structures, offering emotional and economic support critical for individual and collective success. In the Black community, where historical challenges have often tested the strength of familial bonds, the institution of marriage becomes a powerful tool for empowerment, nurturing resilience, and fostering a sense of identity and belonging.

Affirmation

I affirm the importance of marriage within my cultural context. I embrace the legacy of strength and resilience that comes from familial bonds. I am committed to seeking a spouse who shares the values and aspirations that empower our community. Through marriage, I contribute to the growth and prosperity of my people."

Criteria to Seek in a Spouse

Cultural Understanding and Respect:

Appreciation and understanding of Black culture involve learning about its history, contributions, and experiences while approaching it with respect and openness. Educate yourself by reading books and articles, watching documentaries and films, following black media, learning history, studying key events, acknowledging contributions, and engaging with black art and culture.

Commitment to Community Empowerment:

A shared passion for community upliftment involves actively contributing to the well-being and growth of your community. Volunteer your time to local organizations, support local businesses, and engage in civic activities. All this shows a willingness to actively contribute to community growth.

Spiritual Foundation:

Shared faith and spiritual beliefs are a delicate process that involves respect, openness, and sensitivity. Live by example since authenticity demonstrates your beliefs through your actions and lifestyles. The positive impact of your faith will inspire others. Recognition of the role of spirituality in family life involves integrating spiritual beliefs and practices. Family discussions on shared beliefs and values help to ensure both of you understand and respect each other.

Biblical Citations

Proverbs 18:22:

"He who finds a wife finds a good thing and obtains favor from the Lord."

Ephesians 5:25:

"Husbands, love your wives, just as Christ also loved the church and gave Himself for her."

1 Corinthians 7:2:

"Nevertheless, because of sexual immorality, let each man have his own wife, and let each woman have her own husband."

Genesis 2:24:

"Therefore a man shall leave his father and mother and be joined to his wife, and they shall become one flesh."

I would like to share my experience as a pastor. We would have a watch night service, and at the end of the service, I would go to my friend's home. Many of the young women from the choir would be there. It was during this time that I would explain the A&B list. I admonished the young women to work and seek Individuals from the B list who loved them and liked to be around them. Let me explain. I would ask them, "Are you dating anyone, and if so, how long have you been dating?" Some would say eight months or two years. Others would say five years. At that point, I would tell them that six months was long enough to decide if this was a worthwhile adventure. Definitely do not give anyone over two years. I also explained that if you cannot walk away from anyone or anything, it has already captured you. I also explained to them that if you cannot walk away from someone you've been with for five years who has not made a commitment to you, then you need to go to the hardware department of Home Depot or Lowe's. When you get there, ask them if they have any knee pads. Because if you have been in a relationship for five years and that person has not committed to you, you will need some knee pads. Many of them took my advice, and many of them were married. Those who did not take the advice would come back three or four years later with regret that they didn't take the advice at that time. Now they've got two or three kids wondering how life is going to be for her and her kids. If you're reading this book, be sure that a person is committed to you, and marriage is a commitment. It's a legal, spiritually binding commitment, and that's what you want if you're seeking a God-given spouse.

Conclusion:

In the Black community, the need for marriage and the search for a life partner go beyond personal fulfillment. It is intertwined with a legacy of strength, resilience, and community empowerment. By embracing the cultural, historical, and biblical foundations, individuals contribute to a narrative of unity and progress within the Black community, ensuring that the institution of marriage remains a source of empowerment and inspiration for generations to come.

Chapter Five:

Traits, Characteristics, and Features to Consider in Finding a Spouse

In earlier chapters, I shared the traits that were important to me as I looked for the perfect spouse. Now, I want to share things you'll need to consider as you find the perfect spouse. Finding a life partner is a significant and personal journey, and what traits are important can vary greatly from person to person. However, there are some commonly considered traits, characteristics, and features that individuals may prioritize when seeking a spouse. Remember that these are general considerations, and personal values and preferences play a crucial role in determining what is important to an individual. Here are some aspects to consider:

Shared Values and Beliefs:

Similar core values and beliefs can be the foundation of a strong and lasting relationship. They are the fundamental principles that guide an individual's actions, decisions, and behavior. They serve as a foundation for guidance and direction, consistency, trust, and integrity.

For example, my wife and I both valued the Christian life, so we attended church together and raised our children with those values. Although she was Catholic and I was Baptist, we agreed to worship in the Baptist church and raise our children there with those Christian values.

Communication Skills:

Effective communication is essential for a healthy relationship. Communication skills are crucial for a personal relationship. They help encompass a range of abilities that help individuals convey information, ideas, and emotions clearly and effectively. These skills include building relationships, clarity and understanding, conflict resolution, collaboration and teamwork, and problem-solving, which are so important in a personal relationship. The ability to express oneself, listen actively, and resolve conflicts is crucial.

Emotional Intelligence:

A partner with emotional intelligence can navigate their own emotions and understand and respond to their partner's emotions effectively. It is the ability to recognize, understand, manage, and influence one's own emotions and the emotions of others. It encompasses a set of skills that contribute to how we perceive and express ourselves, develop and maintain social relationships, cope with challenges, and make decisions. It is the ability to recognize and understand our own emotions, strengths, and weaknesses. In self-awareness, individuals are conscious of how their feelings affect others. Emotional intelligence is essential for a good relationship.

Trustworthiness and Honesty:

Trust is a cornerstone of a successful marriage. Honesty and integrity are vital for building and maintaining trust. Trustworthiness and honesty are fundamental and ethical qualities that are essential for building and maintaining a strong, healthy relationship, both personally and professionally. Trustworthiness refers to the ability to be relied upon as honest and truthful. Reliability is being dependable and consistent in actions and behavior so people can count on a trustworthy person to do what they say they will do. Loyalty demonstrates a

Traits, Characteristics, and Features to Consider 43

commitment to others, whether it is individuals, groups, or organizations. This involves being faithful and supportive, which is what you are looking for in a mate.

Respect and Mutual Support:

Respect and mutual support are key components of positive relationships, fostering an environment of understanding, cooperation, and trust. Respect involves recognizing and valuing the worth, rights, feelings, and qualities of your partner. It means you must acknowledge their contributions, opinions, and presence and value their perspectives. Mutual support refers to the reciprocal provision of assistance, encouragement, and care between two individuals. Key aspects would include collaboration, encouragement, assistance, empathy, and understanding. Respect and mutual support in marriage are important: they strengthen the bond between the two, enhance communication between the two, build trust while giving the ability to navigate challenges, and foster growth by prioritizing respect and mutual support. Couples can create a strong, resilient and loving marriage relationship that would stand the test of time.

Similar Life Goals:

Having similar life goals in marriage can significantly enhance the relationship by allowing the couple's visions and aspirations while fostering deeper connections and cooperation. Strengthening the partnership in a unified direction when both partners share similar goals allows them to move in the same direction, making it easier to plan for the future together. This unity helps in setting and achieving long-term goals, increasing cooperation, sharing common objectives, and encouraging teamwork and collaboration. This enhances communication, and similar goals facilitate open and effective communication. Couples can discuss their strategies, move freely while understanding each other's perspective, and work together toward common aims. Having similar life goals in marriage can significantly enhance the relationship.

Financial Compatibility:

Similar attitudes towards money, financial goals, and spending habits can reduce potential sources of conflict. Financial compatibility in marriage refers to aligning attitudes, values, and practices related to money management between the partners. It is crucial for maintaining harmony and stability in the relationship. Shared financial goals and values should be the common objectives, with both partners agreeing on short-term and long-term financial goals such as saving for a home, retirement, children's education, or travel. Shared financial values are important for savings and debt management. This requires effective communication, open and regular dialogue, and honest discussions about finances, including income expenses, debt, and financial plans. Agreeing upon a budget and creating and sticking to one that reflects both partners' needs and preferences involves tackling income and expenses and making joint decisions on discretionary spending.

Sense of Humor:

Shared humor and the ability to find joy in similar things can contribute to a positive and enjoyable relationship. A sense of humor refers to the ability of partners to find joy and laughter together using humor to enhance their relationship. It involves sharing jokes, light-hearted moments, and being able to laugh at oneself. This strengthens the bonds between the two, sharing moments of laughter, creating positive memories, and strengthening the emotional connection between the parties. It fosters a sense of camaraderie and intimacy. Humor can be a way to express affection and show understanding, deepening the

Traits, Characteristics, and Features to Consider   45

emotional bond between the two. Using humor can diffuse tense situations and make difficult conversations more manageable. It helps break the ice and makes discussions less confrontational. Humor can be a subtle and effective way to express thoughts and feelings that might be difficult to communicate directly it softens the delivery of sensitive topics. Couples who share a sense of humor often approach life with a more positive outlook. This positivity can help them navigate challenges and setbacks more effectively. Laughing together reduces stress and promotes relaxation. It releases endorphins, which improve mood and overall wellness.

Problem-Solving Skills:

A partner who can collaborate in problem-solving rather than placing blame can contribute to a healthier relationship dynamic. Problem-solving skills in marriage involve effectively addressing and resolving conflict, making decisions together, and navigating challenges as a team. Key aspects include open, honest, and respectful communication, which is crucial. Both parties need to express their thoughts and feelings clearly and listen actively to each other. Empathy is understanding and valuing each other's perspectives and emotions, which helps in finding mutually acceptable solutions. Compromise is where both parties should be willing to give and take, finding a middle ground where both feel satisfied with the outcome. Patience allows time for emotions to cool and for thoughtful consideration of solutions rather than rushing to a resolution. Creativity thinking outside the box to find new solutions or approaches that might have been considered before. Decision-making is evaluating opinions together, considering the pros and cons, and making decisions that are best for the relationship as a whole. Problem-solving is finding alternative solutions and being open to trying different approaches when facing challenges. Developing these skills can help couples constructively handle disputes, maintain a strong connection, and build a lasting, resilient partnership.

Adaptability and Flexibility:

Life is unpredictable, and the ability to adapt to changes and be flexible in various situations can be valuable. Adaptability and flexibility in marriage refer to the ability of partners to adjust to changes and challenges that arise over time. Adaptability is embracing change, being open to changes in circumstances, roles, and expectations, and adjusting one's behavior or mindset accordingly. Handling uncertainty is managing the unknown or unexpected events calmly and finding ways to navigate through them together. Learning and growing is being willing to learn from experiences and grow as individuals and as a couple adapting to strategies and approaches as needed. Flexibility is adjusting expectations and being willing to modify one's expectations or plans based on new information or circumstances. Accommodating each other is adjusting one's behavior or plans to accommodate the needs and preferences of the partner and vice versa. In essence, adaptability and flexibility help couples manage life's inevitable changes and challenges more effectively while fostering a harmonious relationship.

Family Values:

Compatibility in terms of family values, including the importance of family relationships and traditions, can contribute to a harmonious home life. Family values refer to the shared principles and beliefs that guide a couple's behavior and decisions regarding their family life. These values often shape the way partners interact with each other, their children, and extended family members. Respect is the ability to argue each other's opinions, boundaries, and individuality while maintaining a supportive and respectful environment. Communication is prioritizing open, honest, and effective communication to resolve conflict, make

Traits, Characteristics, and Features to Consider 47

decisions, and express needs. Trust is building and maintaining mutual confidence in one another through honesty, reliability, and transparency. Family time values and prioritizes time spent together while creating opportunities for bonding and shared experiences. Traditions and culture are respecting and incorporating culture, religion, and family traditions that are important to both partners and their families. By allowing these values to be applied, couples can strengthen their marriage and create a cohesive and supportive family environment.

Shared Interests and Hobbies:

While it is not necessary, having some common interests or hobbies can provide shared activities and bonding opportunities. We both believed in our political system in this country and that we would work for the best candidate, whether it was a Democrat or a Republican, but we would serve and work with the candidate of our choice. Working on the campaigns brought us closer together because we enjoy working together. Additionally, we enjoyed the hobby of playing cards and we enjoyed playing cards with other couples. We would play Pinochle, and we would play Bridge with Hearts, Spades, and a variety of cards, which brought shared values and interests together along with the hobbies.

Independence:

Allowing each other space for individual growth and maintaining a level of independence within the relationship is crucial. Cathy enjoyed her sorority groups and would do various church projects with the women. This brought a great level of independence to her. She was able to lead and guide the women and organize them in ways, and I saw professional growth as well as camaraderie and independence. This was a great thing for me. I enjoyed playing cards with the guys, and she gave me space to do that. We would play cards half the night, and I enjoyed the growth. I knew it was my time to host the games that brought independence and growth, and we both grew individually.

Physical and Mental Well-being:

Prioritizing health and well-being, both physically and mentally, contributes to a fulfilling and sustainable relationship. Physical and mental well-being includes consuming a balanced diet with the right portions of fruit, vegetables, and proteins for optimum health. Exercising regularly and engaging in physical activities like walking supported our cardiovascular health. Cathy would also make certain that we got seven hours of sleep every night, and of course, we maintained that schedule as much as possible. I think all of this contributes to individuals' physical and mental well-being.

Remember that these traits are not exhaustive, and personal preferences may lead individuals to prioritize different qualities. Open communication and a willingness to understand each other's needs and values are key to building a strong foundation for a successful marriage.

Chapter Six:

Embracing One Another Before Marriage

In the journey towards marriage, embracing one another is a crucial and delicate period that demands careful consideration of physical and emotional intimacy. Choosing abstinence or navigating the path of physical intimacy requires thoughtful reflection guided by personal values, respect, and a commitment to the principles laid out in the Bible.

The Power of Emotional Connection

Building a strong emotional connection is paramount before delving into physical intimacy. Open communication, understanding, and shared values create a foundation for a healthy and lasting relationship.

The power of emotional connection is profound and plays a significant role in various aspects of human life, including relationships, communication, decision-making, and overall well-being. Here are some key points that highlight the importance and impact of emotional connections.

Relationships and Social Bonds:

Emotional connections form the foundation of strong, meaningful relationships. Whether with family, friends, or romantic partners, the ability to understand and resonate with each other's emotions strengthens the bond. Emotional connections foster trust, empathy, and mutual understanding, creating a supportive environment for individuals.

Communication

Emotions are a crucial component of effective communication. People are more likely to remember and respond positively to messages that evoke emotional reactions.

Emotional connection in communication helps convey sincerity and authenticity, making interactions more engaging and relatable.

Motivation and Inspiration

Emotional connections can be powerful motivators. When individuals feel a deep emotional connection to a goal or a cause, they are more likely to invest time and effort to achieve it. Inspirational leaders often leverage emotional connections to rally teams and communities around a shared vision or purpose.

Decision-Making:

Emotions play a significant role in decision-making. People often choose based on their feelings about the options rather than solely relying on logic. Brands and businesses recognize the power of emotional connections in consumer decision-making, using emotional appeals in advertising and marketing strategies.

Personal Well-Being:

Strong emotional connections contribute to overall well-being. Feeling connected to others provides a sense of belonging and support, reducing stress and promoting mental and emotional health. Positive emotional connections can enhance resilience, helping individuals cope with life's challenges more effectively.

Creativity and Innovation:

Emotional connections can fuel creativity and innovation. Collaborative environments where individuals feel emotionally connected and safe to express themselves often lead to more innovative ideas and solutions.

Loyalty

In the business world, emotional connections are crucial for building customer loyalty. Companies that prioritize customer relationships, understand their needs, and connect with them emotionally are more likely to retain loyal customers. The same is true in marriage. Emotional connections are vital. Your spouse will need you to prioritize their needs and connect with them.

Learning and Memory:

Emotions influence the way we process and remember information. Content that elicits emotional responses tends to be more memorable and impactful.

Educational experiences that incorporate emotional elements can enhance learning and retention.

In summary, the power of emotional connection is pervasive and influences various aspects of human life. Developing and nurturing emotional connections can lead to more fulfilling relationships, effective communication, and a greater sense of purpose and well-being. Whether in personal or professional spheres, recognizing and valuing the emotional dimension of human experiences can lead to positive outcomes and enriched lives.

Choosing Abstinence

Abstinence before marriage is a choice deeply rooted in the commitment to honor oneself, one's partner, and the sanctity of marriage. **1 Thessalonians 4:3-5** speaks to the importance of sexual purity: *"For this is the will of God, your* *sanctification: that you should abstain from sexual immorality; that each of you should know how to possess his own vessel in sanctification and honor, not in passion of lust, like the Gentiles who do not know God."*

Choosing abstinence refers to the decision to abstain from certain activities or behaviors, typically in the context of refraining from sexual activity. While the term is often associated with abstaining from sexual intercourse until marriage, it can also extend to abstaining from other behaviors, such as substance abuse or certain types of relationships. Here are some reasons why individuals might choose abstinence:

Personal Values

Many people choose abstinence based on their personal or religious beliefs. Some religions promote abstinence until marriage to uphold certain moral or ethical values.

Health Concerns

Abstinence can be a choice driven by health considerations, such as avoiding the risk of sexually transmitted infections (STIs) or unintended pregnancies. It is a form of contraception that doesn't involve the use of contraceptives.

Emotional Well-being

Some individuals choose abstinence to prioritize their emotional well-being. They may believe that engaging in sexual activity should be reserved for a committed relationship or marriage, where emotional intimacy is well-established.

Focus on Personal Development

Individuals may choose abstinence to focus on personal development, education, or career goals without the potential distractions or complications that can arise from sexual relationships.

Cultural or Societal Expectations:

Cultural or societal norms and expectations can also influence the decision to abstain from certain behaviors. In some cultures, abstinence until marriage is strongly encouraged.

Fear of Consequences:

Fear of negative consequences, such as unintended pregnancies or the emotional toll of casual relationships, can be a factor in choosing abstinence.

It's important to note that choosing abstinence is a personal decision, and individuals may have various reasons for making this choice. Respecting one's own values, beliefs, and boundaries is essential in making decisions about personal relationships and behaviors. Additionally, communication and mutual understanding are crucial in relationships where partners may have different views on abstinence.

Establishing Boundaries

Clearly defining physical boundaries is essential in maintaining purity and respecting each other's journey. **Ephesians 5:3** encourages believers to avoid even a hint of sexual immorality: *"But fornication and all uncleanness or covetousness, let it not even be named among you, as is fitting for saints."*

The Power of Affirmation

"I affirm the importance of building a strong emotional connection before marriage. I choose to embrace my partner with respect and honor, acknowledging the sacredness of physical intimacy within the commitment of marriage. My choices align with God's principles for purity, love, and respect."

Chapter Seven:

Summation of Benefits in Waiting for YOUR Spouse

Waiting for the right spouse can have various benefits that contribute to a healthier and more fulfilling long-term relationship. Here are some key advantages:

Emotional Maturity:

Waiting allows individuals to develop emotional maturity and a better understanding of themselves. This maturity is essential for handling the complexities of a committed relationship.

Personal Growth:

During the waiting period, individuals can focus on personal growth, pursuing their goals, and developing a strong sense of identity. This contributes to a more well-rounded and confident person entering a relationship.

Clarity of Values:

Taking time before committing yourself to a spouse allows for a clearer understanding of personal values and priorities. This clarity is crucial for finding a compatible partner who shares similar values.

Established Career and Stability:

Waiting often involves building a stable foundation in terms of career and financial stability. This can lead to a more secure and comfortable environment for a relationship to flourish.

Better Decision-Making:

Waiting allows individuals to make relationship decisions based on wisdom and experience rather than impulsiveness. This can lead to a more thoughtful partner selection and a stronger foundation for the relationship.

Increased Compatibility:

Waiting allows individuals to understand themselves better and, as a result, find someone with whom they are genuinely compatible. This can lead to a more harmonious and lasting relationship.

Reduced Pressure:

Waiting eliminates the societal pressure to conform to a specific timeline for finding a spouse. This can lead to more authentic and less rushed relationship decisions.

Stronger Communication Skills:

The time spent waiting can be used to enhance communication skills, an essential aspect of any successful relationship. Effective communication is crucial for resolving conflicts and maintaining a healthy connection.

Healthy Relationship Expectations:

Waiting allows individuals to develop realistic expectations for a relationship, avoiding the pitfalls of idealized or unrealistic notions of love and partnership.

Increased Self-Confidence:

Building a strong sense of self-worth and confidence during the waiting period can contribute to a healthier and more equal partnership, where both individuals bring a positive self-image to the relationship.

Summation of Benefits in Waiting for Your Spouse

Remember that everyone's journey is unique, and there is no one-size-fits-all approach to finding a spouse. The key is to prioritize self-discovery, personal growth, and building a foundation that supports a fulfilling and lasting partnership.

Chapter Eight:

Seven Steps to Find Your Spouse from God

In this chapter, I will summarize each chapter to assist those seeking God's choice for a spouse. You will notice that I repeat several of the principles. That's on purpose! Our communities have become so accustomed to living opposite God's divine order that we need to hear it multiple times just to make it part of our thinking about marriage. If you truly desire *your* divine spouse, not just any spouse, take your time. Study each recommendation as you discuss your desire for life-long, committed companionship with God.

Chapter 1: The Foundation of Divine Love

Seek God First: Establish a strong relationship with God before seeking a life partner. Matthew 6:33 emphasizes the importance of prioritizing God's kingdom above all.

The Lord as Shepherd: Psalm 23:1 describes God as the shepherd who guides and provides for us, just as He will guide us to a suitable spouse.

Delight in the Lord: Psalm 37:4 reminds us that when we find joy in God, He aligns our desires with His will, including the choice of a spouse.

Unity in Companionship: Ecclesiastes 4:9-12 highlights the strength of a relationship grounded in God, where both partners support and uplift each other.

Be Equally Yoked: 2 Corinthians 6:14 warns of the importance of being spiritually compatible with a partner to avoid discord in faith and values.

Commitment to God's Timing: Waiting for God's guidance in finding a partner ensures the relationship is built on a solid spiritual foundation.

Foundation of Love: A thriving relationship with God prepares us for a loving, committed marriage while strengthening the bond with a divine spouse.

Chapter 2: The Biblical Basis for Finding Your Spouse

God's Plan for Companionship: Genesis 2:18 shows God's intention for humans to have partners, emphasizing companionship as a divine design.

Trust in God's Guidance: Proverbs 3:5-6 encourages trusting God fully in the process of finding a spouse, ensuring His wisdom directs our paths.

Patience in Waiting: Psalm 27:14 advises waiting on the Lord for His perfect timing in bringing the right spouse into our lives.

Seek Righteousness: Proverbs 31:10 advises finding a spouse whose character reflects godly virtues, focusing on spiritual alignment rather than external factors.

Discernment through Prayer: Philippians 1:9-10 emphasizes the importance of praying for discernment in finding a spouse whose values align with God's.

Commitment to God's Will: A relationship rooted in God's principles helps ensure that the partnership reflects His love and righteousness.

Faithful Waiting: Seeking God's direction in finding a spouse through prayer and trusting in His timing brings peace and fulfillment.

Chapter 3: Finding My Spouse with Divine Guidance

Foundation of Faith: A strong foundation in faith, nurtured from childhood, was key in the journey toward finding a spouse.

Praying for Specific Qualities: Creating a list of desired qualities in a spouse and presenting it to God in prayer helps articulate your needs to the Divine.

Overcoming Trials: Personal experiences, such as a failed marriage, can lead to deeper reliance on God's guidance in finding a supportive partner.

Divine Encounters: Spiritual experiences, like the one with Pastor Harris, provide affirmation and clarity in pursuing a relationship.

Reconnection with God's Plan: Unexpected meetings and spiritual confirmations reinforce that the journey to love is divinely guided.

Faith in Action: Taking active steps, such as engaging in church and prayer, strengthens the spiritual connection with the future spouse.

Union in Faith: The shared spiritual experience confirms that the relationship is divinely ordained and solidified by faith.

Chapter 4: The Significance of Marriage and Finding a Spouse in the Community.

Historical Legacy: Marriage in the Black community carries deep historical and cultural significance, serving as a source of strength and resilience.

Cultural Empowerment: Strong family structures and marriages contribute to empowerment, stability, and growth within the community.

Spiritual Foundations: Shared faith and spiritual beliefs within the marriage foster unity, guiding couples to navigate challenges with biblical values.

Respect for Culture: Appreciating and understanding Black cultural heritage is essential in finding a spouse who respects shared values and traditions.

Commitment to Community Growth: A spouse should share in the commitment to uplift the community and contribute to collective progress.

Marriage as Empowerment: In the Black community, marriage is not just about personal fulfillment but also about strengthening cultural and family bonds.

Biblical Guidance: Scripture serves as a guide in understanding the importance of marriage, ensuring that relationships honor God and strengthen the community.

Chapter 5: Traits, Characteristics, and Features to Consider in Finding a Spouse

Shared Values: Having similar core values and beliefs is foundational for a strong and lasting marriage.

Communication Skills: Effective communication is essential for expressing emotions, resolving conflicts, and maintaining a healthy relationship.

Emotional Intelligence: A spouse with emotional intelligence can navigate their own and their partner's emotions, creating a nurturing and understanding relationship.

Trust and Honesty: Trustworthiness and honesty form the bedrock of a successful relationship, ensuring mutual respect and integrity.

Mutual Respect and Support: Both partners should respect each other's individuality and support one another's growth and aspirations.

Shared Goals: Having similar life goals, particularly regarding family, finances, and career, helps build a unified vision for the future.

Adaptability and Flexibility: Life is unpredictable, so the ability to adapt and be flexible is key to maintaining harmony in the marriage.

Chapter 6: Embracing One Another Before Marriage

Emotional Connection First: Building a strong emotional connection before marriage creates a healthy foundation for the relationship.

Choosing Abstinence: Abstinence before marriage is a commitment to purity, honoring God's principles of sanctity in relationships.

Establishing Boundaries: Clear physical boundaries help maintain respect and purity in the relationship, protecting both partners.

Affirming God's Principles: Choosing to align with biblical principles regarding purity ensures that the relationship is built on respect and love.

Honoring the Sanctity of Marriage: By delaying physical intimacy, couples honor the sacredness of marriage and commit to God's design.

Communication of Values: Openly discussing values and expectations regarding physical and emotional intimacy strengthens trust and understanding.

Respect for the Journey: Embracing one another with respect and love during the journey toward marriage reflects God's plan for a fulfilling partnership.

Chapter 7: Closing – The Benefits of Waiting for Your Spouse

Emotional Maturity: Waiting allows individuals to develop emotional maturity, essential for a healthy and lasting marriage.

Personal Growth: Focusing on personal goals and growth during the waiting period leads to stronger, more confident individuals entering the relationship.

Clarity of Values: Taking time before committing ensures that you have a clear understanding of personal values and priorities in a spouse.

Better Decision-Making: Waiting fosters better decision-making based on wisdom and experience, leading to a stronger relationship.

Established Stability: Achieving financial and career stability creates a solid foundation for a flourishing marriage.

Increased Compatibility: Waiting can help you better understand yourself, which can lead to finding someone who is truly compatible with your values and goals.

Authentic Partnership: Waiting eliminates pressure, allowing for more authentic relationships based on mutual love and respect rather than societal expectations.

In conclusion, I have shared the key elements I experienced as a man who was blessed to find and marry the perfect mate for me. It is my sincere prayer regarding your quest for a divine spouse that after fervent prayer and following the leading of God's Spirit, you will find God's choice for you, and the two of you will have a harmonious and fruitful life together – as one.

Author Bio

Reverend David L. Roberson has been responding to God's call on his life to preach the gospel since May 20, 1980. He was then ordained to the Gospel Ministry on May 20, 1983, at New Prospect Baptist Church in Detroit, MI, under the leadership of Reverend S.L. Whitney. He founded and organized the Spirit Field Baptist Church in 1980 with approximately 100 members. In 1992, Pastor Roberson was called to serve as the Pastor of New Hope Missionary Baptist Church in Southfield, MI. God envisioned him with a seven-point plan that would assist the church with its growth.

One of Pastor Roberson's favorite biblical quotations is Proverbs 29:18: *"Where there is no vision, the people perish."* With the power of God, his vision unfolded, and when he left the church, the membership had grown from 99 to over 3000.

Acquiring the following degrees, Pastor Roberson has sought every opportunity to grow and be equipped for all that God calls him to do.

Education Accomplishments

Reverend Roberson has an Associate of Arts Degree from Wayne County Community College in Wayne County, Michigan.

Reverend Roberson has a Bachelor of Science Degree from Central Michigan University in Detroit, MI.

Reverend Roberson has a Master of Arts Degree from the University of Detroit in Detroit, MI.

Reverend Roberson has a Doctorate of the Ministry Degree from the Ecumenical Theological Seminary in Detroit, MI.

To contact Pastor Roberson for speaking engagements, interviews, etc., please contact him at:

David L. Roberson
www.FindYourDivineSpouse.com
divinespouse1@gmail.com

www.ingramcontent.com/pod-product-compliance
Lightning Source LLC
Chambersburg PA
CBHW011408070526
44586CB00021B/2583